WASP and other PLAYS

by

STEVE MARTIN

SAMUEL FRENCH, INC.
45 West 25th Street   NEW YORK 10010
7623 Sunset Boulevard HOLLYWOOD 90046
LONDON   TORONTO

Wasp and Other Plays © 1998 by 40 Share Productions, Inc.
"Wasp" © 1994, 1995, 1996 by 40 Share Productions, Inc.
" The Zig-Zag Woman" and "Patter for the Floating Lady" © 1996 by
40 Share Productions, Inc.

ALL RIGHTS RESERVED

CAUTION: Professionals and amateurs are hereby warned that WASP AND OTHER PLAYS is subject to a royalty. It is fully protected under the copyright laws of the United States of America, the British Commonwealth, including Canada, and all other countries of the Copyright Union. All rights, including professional, amateur, motion pictures, recitation, lecturing, public reading, radio broadcasting, television, and the rights of translation into foreign languages are strictly reserved. In its present form the play is dedicated to the reading public only.

The amateur live stage performance rights to WASP AND OTHER PLAYS are controlled exclusively by Samuel French, Inc. and royalty arrangements and licenses must be secured well in advance of presentation. PLEASE NOTE that amateur royalty fees are set upon application in accordance with your producing circumstances. When applying for a royalty quotation and license please give us the number of performances intended, dates of production, your seating capacity and admission fee. Royalties are payable one week before the opening performance of the play to Samuel French, Inc., at 45 W. 25th Street, New York, NY 10010; or at 7623 Sunset Blvd., Hollywood, CA 90046, or to Samuel French (Canada), Ltd.,100 Lombard Street, Toronto, Ontario, Canada M5C 1M3.

Royalty of the required amount must be paid whether the play is presented for charity or gain and whether or not admission is charged.

Stock royalty quoted on application to Samuel French, Inc.

For all other rights than those stipulated above, apply to International Creative Management, 40 W. 57th Street New York, NY 10019.

Particular emphasis is laid on the question of amateur or professional readings, permission and terms for which must be secured in writing from Samuel French, Inc.

Copying from this book in whole or in part is strictly forbidden by law, and the right of performance is not transferable.

Whenever the play is produced the following notice must appear on all programs, printing and advertising for the play: "Produced by special arrangement with Samuel French, Inc."

Due authorship credit must be given on all programs, printing and advertising for the play.

ISBN 0 573 60311 1   Printed in the U.S.A.

No one shall commit or authorize any act or omission by which the copyright of, or the right to copyright, this play may be impaired.

No one shall make any changes in this play for the purpose of production.

Publication of this play does not imply availability for performance. Both amateurs and professionals considering a production are *strongly* advised in their own interests to apply to Samuel French, Inc., for written permission before starting rehearsals, advertising, or booking a theater.

No part of this book may be reproduced, stored in a retrieval system, or transmitted in any form, by any means, now known or yet to be invented, including mechanical, electronic, photocopying, recording, videotaping, or otherwise, without the prior written permission of the publisher.

IMPORTANT BILLING AND CREDIT REQUIREMENTS

All producers of WASP AND OTHER PLAYS *must* give credit to the Author of the Play in all programs distributed in connection with performances of the Play and in all instances in which the title of the Play appears for purposes of advertising, publicizing or otherwise exploiting the Play and/or a production. The name of the Author *must* also appear on a separate line, on which no other name appears, immediately following the title, and *must* appear in size of type not less than fifty percent the size of the title type.

TABLE OF CONTENTS

WASP 5

THE ZIG-ZAG WOMAN 39

PATTER FOR THE FLOATING LADY 55

GUILLOTINE 67

WASP

WASP was originally presented by the Ensemble Studio Theatre, Curt Dempster, Artistic Director, Kevin Confoy, Executive Producer, with the following cast:

Dad	Jack Gilpin
Mom	Cecilia de Wolf
Sis	Melinda Hamilton
Son	Josh Soboslai
Female Voice	Jenny O'Hara
Premier, Roger	Richmond Hoxie

Director: **Curt Dempster**
Assistant Director: **Eileen Myers**
Set Designer: **Kert F. Lundell**
Lighting Designer: **Greg MacPherson**
Costume Designer: **Julie Diyle**
Sound Designer: **Jeffrey M. Taylor**
Stage Manager: **Heather Robinson**
Production Stage Manager: **Greeg Fletcher**

. . . .

WASP was presented by the New York Stage and Film Company in Association with the Weissberger Theater Group, RJK Productions, and the Powerhouse Theater at Vassar, August 3, 1994. The cast included:

Dad	Peter Frechette
Mom	Jane Kaczmarek
Sis	Catherine Kellner
Son	Rob Campbell
Female Voice	C. C. Loveheart
Premier, Roger	Frank Raiter

Director: **Barry Edelstein**
Set Designer: **Christine Jones**
Costume Designer: **Laura Cunningham**
Lighting Designer: **Howard Werner**
Sound Designer: **Darren Clark**
Stage Manager: **Sandi Johnson**

....

WASP's original New York production was by the New York Shakespeare Festival, George C. Wolfe, Producer, with the following cast:

Dad	Don McManus
Mom	Carol Kane
Sis	Amelia Campbell
Son	Kevin Isola
Female Voice	Peggy Pope
Premier, Choirmaster, Roger	Nesbitt Blaisdell

Director: **Barry Edelstein**
Scenic Designer: **Thomas Lynch**
Lighting Designer: **Donald Holder**
Costume Designer: **Laura Cunningham**
Sound Designer: **Red Ramona**
Production Stage Manager: **James Latus**

THE ZIG-ZAG WOMAN was originally presented in workshop by the New York Stage and Film Company and the Powerhouse Theater in association with RJK Productions. The cast included:

> Rob Campbell
> Bill Irwin
> Frank Raiter
> Kimberly Williams

> Director: **Barry Edelstein**
> Stage Manager: **Sandi Johnson**

....

The ZIG-ZAG WOMAN's original New York production was by the New York Shakespeare Festival, George C. Wolfe, Producer, with the following cast:

The Zig-Zag Woman	Amelia Campbell
Older Man	Nesbitt Blaisdell
Middle Man	Don McManus
Young Man	Kevin Isola

> Director: **Barry Edelstein**
> Scenic Designer: **Thomas Lynch**
> Lighting Designer: **Donald Holder**
> Costume Designer: **Laura Cunningham**
> Sound Designer: **Red Ramona**
> Production Stage Manager: **James Latus**

WASP

Scene 1

(A kitchen in a fifties' house. A dining table is center stage, with four chairs around it. MOM sets the table in silence. Around the table are DAD, SON, and SIS. MOM sits.)

DAD. Oh God in heaven, which is seventeen miles above the Earth, bless this food grown on this Earth that is four thousand three hundred twenty-five years old. Amen

(They pantomime eating. We hear loud, amplified, prerecorded chewing sounds.)

SON. Jim, where's heaven'?
DAD. Son, it's seventeen miles above the Earth. You enter through clouds. Behind the clouds, there are thirteen golden steps leading to a vestibule. Inside the vestibule is Saint Peter. Next to the vestibule are gates twenty-seven feet high. They are solid god but with an off-center hinge for easy opening.
SON. Then heaven's closer than the moon?
DAD. What do you mean?

SON. Well, according to my science teacher, the moon is 250,000 miles away.

(There is a moment of silence while they contemplate this. MOM bursts into tears. DAD stares at SON and starts to chew. Sounds of loud chewing for a long time.)

SON. Jim, if Adam and Eve were the first people on Earth and they had two sons, where did everybody else come from?
DAD. Huh?

(MOM stares at SON.)

SON. Well, if there were only two sons, then who did they marry and where did everybody else come from?

(Another moment of silence. MOM bursts into tears.)

DAD. Do you like your science teacher?
SON. Yeah.
DAD. Well, that's too bad because he's going to have his tongue pierced in hell by a hot poker.

(The phone rings. SIS looks up in anticipation, grips the table.)

SIS. Oh, my God, it's Jeremy!

(MOM goes to the wall phone and answers:)

MOM. Oh, hi, June!... *(SIS dies when she realizes it's not it's not for her.)* Uh-huh... yeah... really? ... REALLY? Good news! Thanks! Bye. *(She hangs up, then to herself:)* Oh, great! Great news for me!

(MOM looks at everyone in anticipation. No one asks her anything. She sits back down.)
(Sounds of loud chewing.)

SIS. Guess what I learned in home economics?

(More munching.)

MOM. I went to a flower show today, and I just thought it was beautiful; they have the most beautiful things there... I went with Miriam and she had been before but there was a new exhibit so...

(DAD starts talking louder and over MOM.)

MOM.	DAD.
She wanted to go again and she knows someone there and she got tickets for me so I got in free. Normally it costs three dollars to go in, so I used the money I saved and picked up a nice arrangement...	(Loud and over MOM:) Boy, oh boy, when I was in college, I remember we used to wear these skinny little pants and shirts with big collars; boy, we must have looked silly.

(MOMS dialogue peters out.)

(The phone rings. SIS looks at the phone in anticipation.)

SIS. *(Frantic.)* It's Jeremy, it's got to be!

(MOM answers it.)

MOM. Hello? Oh. Jim, it's for you. It's Mr. Carlyle.

(SIS collapses again.)

DAD. I'll take it in the living room.

(DAD exits. Big relax from the family.)

DAD. *(Offstage, loud and muffled:)* I don't give a damn what they're talking about if they can't meet us halfway then we've got to reconsider the whole arrangement. There's no sense in doing what we talked about unless we're willing to do it without a contract and I don't want to see the situation turn around unless we want it to turn around...

(During the speech, MOM, SIS, and SON begin to quake, rattling dishes and cutlery. MOM starts to clear dishes, shaking her way with cups and saucers to the sink. DAD emits a cheery laugh; the family relaxes.)

SON. *(Relieved, trying to make conversation:)* Where's the dog?
SIS. Yeah, what happened to Coco? I haven't seen her in about two days. And it's not like she comes back at night; the food's always left in the dish.

MOM. She just wouldn't stay off the furniture so I put her to sleep.

(SIS stares horrified into space. DAD returns, sits.)

DAD. Where's Grandmom? We haven't heard from her in about a week.

(SIS and SON look horrified at MOM. MOM looks guilty, shifts uncomfortably.)

MOM. *(Then:)* In Europe they eat the salad after the main course, and that's what we're doing tonight.
DAD. *(Incredulous:)* Salad *after* the main course?
SON. Weird.
MOM. Here it is...

(MOM brings out a huge cherry Jell-O ring with fruit bits on it.)

DAD. *(Looks into the cherry ring and points to a piece of fruit:)* What's that on top?
MOM. Mango.

(SON stifles a vomit.)

SIS. Eyew. I don't think I want any salad. May I be excused? I have to go to choir molestation.
MOM. Okay, you run off.
DAD. I'll have a little piece.

(DAD takes a piece, carefully cutting around and avoiding the mango. MOM starts to cut a piece for SON.)

SON. I don't think I want any either, Mom.

(DAD glares at him.)

SON. Okay, just a little piece. (He bows his head and utters to himself:) No mango, no mango, no mango...

(MOM carefully cuts him a piece. SON's eyes widen in terror as she gives him the piece with the mango in it. He thinks about it for a second and starts rubbing his forehead rapidly back and forth with his hand. He continues to do this during next dialogue. MOM takes out a letter and sets it nervously on the table.)

DAD. What's that?
MOM. *(Nervous:)* It's a letter from the chamber of commerce.
SON. *(Finishes rubbing his forehead:)* Mom, can I be excused? I feel like I have a temperature.
MOM. *(Feels his forehead with the back of her hand:)* My, oh my, you sure do. You better go straight to bed.

(SON disappears quickly, not having to eat his mango.)

MOM. *(As he goes:)* Do you want to take your salad to your room?

(SON indicates he has a stomachache too.)

DAD. What's it about?

MOM. Well, you know our lawn jockey?

DAD. Yeah.

MOM. They want us to paint its face white.

DAD. Why on earth would they want us to do that?

MOM. They feel it's offensive to some of the Negroes in the community.

DAD. That's like saying there never was such a thing as a Negro lawn jockey. It's really a celebration of the great profession of lawn jockeying.

MOM. They think it shows prejudice.

DAD. Well, that's ridiculous. Some of my best friends are Negro. Jerry at work is a Negro, and we work side by side without the slightest problem.

MOM. That's true; he is a Negro. Well, he's a Navajo.

DAD. But times have changed. I'll make a compromise with them. I'll paint the nineteen jockeys on the north side of the driveway white, but I'm leaving the nineteen on the other side of the driveway alone, and I'm not touching the six on the porch.

MOM. That sounds fair. Jim, I have something to discuss with you. Maybe you can help. Lately, I've been having feelings of... distance. My heart will start racing, and I feel like I'm going to die. I don't like to leave the house, because when I get to the supermarket, I always start to feel terrified...

(SIS, dressed for choir, enters with the evening paper.)

SIS. Evening paper's here.

(SIS exits.)

DAD. Thanks, Judy... uh, Sandy.

(SIS turns away. It says KATHY on the back of her choir robe. DAD takes the paper, spreads it open, covering his face, and starts to read silently.)

MOM. *(Continuing:)* My mouth gets dry... my palms get moist, and I feel like... like I'm going to die. *(She continues as though nothing is different.)* And when I don't feel that way, I spend most of the day in fear that the feeling is going to come over me. Sometimes I hear things. I don't think I can live like this.

DAD. *(From behind paper:)* Honey, it sounds to me like you're having symptoms of fear without knowing what is it you're afraid of. I'm not going to pretend to know how to cure something like that, but I want you to know that I will be beside you while we together figure out how to conquer this thing. I appreciate how difficult your job is around this house. You are deeply loved. I admire you as a person, as well as a wife. I'm interested in what you say and if there's anytime you need me, I will stop everything to help you.

MOM. Oh, my God, Jim.

(MOM is moved. DAD leans over to kiss her, and although he still holds the newspaper in front of his face, he kisses her through it. It's a tender smooch and he's so moved, he closes his arms around her head, still holding the newspaper. Her head is completely encircled in it. They break.)

DAD. *(Still holding newspaper:)* Hmmm. You still get me excited. *(He brings down paper.)* Now why don't you pour us

a drink, and I'll meet you upstairs?
MOM. Oh! Oh yes...

(DAD exits. MOM goes to the cupboard, removes a cocktail shaker, throws in some ingredients, shakes it. She takes out two glasses, one a tiny shot glass, the other glass tankard size. She pours the drink in the tiny glass, then in the large one. She picks up the two drinks, starts to exit, then walks center.)

MOM. *(To the air:)* Voices?
FEMALE VOICE. *(Offstage:)* Yes?
MOM. Hello.
FEMALE VOICE. Hello, Diane.
MOM. Would you visit me if things were different?
FEMALE VOICE. There would be no need.
MOM. Does heaven exist?
FEMALE VOICE. No.
MOM. Does hell exist?
FEMALE VOICE. No.
MOM. Well, that's something anyway. Do things work out in the end?
FEMALE VOICE. No.
MOM. Am I still pretty?
FEMALE VOICE. *(Pause while she thinks:)* Happiness will make you beautiful.
MOM. You've made me feel better. *(She starts to go, then:)* Voices?...
FEMALE VOICE. Yes.?
MOM. Is there a heartland?
FEMALE VOICE. Yes.

MOM. Could I go there?
FEMALE VOICE. You're in it.
MOM. Oh. Does the human heart exist?
FEMALE VOICE. Listen, you can hear them breaking.
MOM. What is melancholy?
FEMALE VOICE. Wouldn't you love to dance with him in the moonlight?
MOM. *(Starts to go, then turns back:)* Voices, when he says he loves me, what does he mean?

(Silence. Lights slowly fade.)

Scene 2
LEPTON

(Lights up. SON's room. We hear MOM's sexual cries coming through the wall. She finishes. Immediately, DAD comes into the room, wearing a robe.)

DAD. *(Holding a doorknob sign that says PRIVATE:)* Private? It's not really private, is it?
SON. No.
DAD. Well, let's not have the yablons. Der fashion rests particularly well. I hop da balloon fer forest waters. Aged well-brood water babies. In der yablons.
SON. Dad, sometimes I don't know what you're talking about.
DAD. Oh yeah, you're too young to understand now, but one day, you'll have response not too fer-well keption.

SON. Jim, do you think I could get a bicycle. How would you pay for it?

SON. Well. I don't know. I was hoping...

DAD. You see, Son, a bicycle is a luxury item. You know what a luxury item is?

SON. No.

DAD. A luxury item is a thing that you have that annoys other people that you have it. Like our very green lawn. That's a luxury item. Oh, it could be less green, I suppose; but that's not what it's about. I work on that lawn, maybe more than I should and pour a little bit o' money into it, but it's a luxury item for me, out there to annoy the others. And let's be fair; they have their luxury items that annoy me. On the corner, that mailbox made out of a ship's chain. Now there's no way I wouldn't like that out in front of our house, but I went for the lawn. What' I'm getting at is that you have to work for a luxury item. So if you want that bicycle, you're going to have to work for it. Now, I've got a little lot downtown that we've had for several years, and if you wanted to go down there on weekends and after school and, say, put up a building on it, I think we could get you that bicycle.

SON. Gosh.

DAD. Yes, I know, you're pretty excited. It's not easy putting up a building, Son, but these are the ancient traditions, handed down from the peoples of Gondwanaland, who lived on the plains of Golgotha. Based upon the precepts of Hammurabi. Written in cuneiform on the gates of Babylon. Deduced from the cryptograms of the Questioner of the sphinx and gleaned from the incunabula of Ratdolt. Delivered unto me by the fleet-footed Mercury when the retrograde Mars backed into Gemini, interpreted from the lyrics of "What a

Swell Party." Appeared on my living room wall in blood writ there by God himself and incised in the Holy Trowel of the Masons. Son, we don't get to talk that much; in fact, as far as I can remember, we've never talked. But I was wondering several years ago, and unfortunately never really got around to asking you until now, I was wondering, what you plan to do with your life?

SON. Well...

DAD. Before you answer, let me just say that I didn't know what I wanted to do with my life until I was twenty-eight. Which is late when you want to be a gymnast, which, by the way, I gave up when I found out it was considered more an art than a sport. But now, your mother and I have seventeen grand in the bank, at today's prices that's like being a millionaire. See, if you've got a dollar and you spend twenty-nine cents on a loaf of bread, you've still got seventeen grand. There's a math lesson for you.

SON. All I know is, it's going to be a great life.

DAD. Well, Son, I have no idea what you're talking about, but I want to suggest that you finish school first and go on to college and get a Ph.D. in Phrenology. But let me just say that no matter what in life you choose to do, I will be there to shame you, unless of course you pass the seventeen thousand mark. Then you will be awarded my college Sigma Delta Phuk-a-lucka pin. Good-bye, and I hope to see you around the house.

(DAD shakes the SON's hand, exits.)

SON. Okay, Dad, I mean, Jim.

(SON stays in the room, takes out a purple pendant, which he puts around his neck. He than takes out a small homemade radio with antenna, dials it. We hear glitches and gwarks, then the sound of a solar wind.)

SON. Premier... Premier... come in, Premier.

(A cheesy spaceman, PREMIER, walks out on the stage.)

PREMIER. Yes?
SON. How are things on Lepton?
PREMIER. Three hundred eight-five degrees Fahrenheit. It rained molten steel. Now that's cold.
SON. Tell me again, okay?
PREMIER. Again?
SON. I need it now.
PREMIER. How long has it been since my first visit?
SON. Ten years.
PREMIER. Ah yes. You were four, and you were granted the Vision.
SON. Yes.
PREMIER. So much is credited to the gene pool these days. But the gene pool is nothing compared to the Vision. It's really what I enjoy doing most. Placing the Vision where it's least expected. Anyway, you need to hear it?
SON. Yes.
PREMIER. All right. Her skin will be rose on white. She will come to you, her face close to yours, her breath on your mouth. She will speak words voicelessly, which you will understand because of the movement of her lips on yours. Her hand will be on the small of your back and her fingers will be

blades. Your blood will pool around you. You will receive a transfusion of a clear liquid that has been exactly measured. That liquid will be sadness. And then, whatever her name may be—Carol, Susan, Virginia—then, she will die, and you will mourn her. Her death will be final in all respects but this: she will be alive and with someone else. But time and again, you will walk in, always at the same age you are now, with your arms open, your heart as big as the moon, not anticipating the total eclipse. They call you a WASP, *but it's women who have the stingers*. However, you will have a gift. A gift so wonderful that it will take you through the days and nights until the end of your life.

SON. I'm getting a gift? What is it?
PREMIER. The desire to work.

(Fade out.)

Scene 3
CHOIR

(Lights up. Choir practice. SIS, wearing her choir robe, stands on a riser. A CHOIRMASTER faces upstage, conducting the rest of the invisible choir.)

SIS. *(Singing:)* I SAW THREE SHIPS A-SAILING IN,
ON CHRISTMAS DAY,
ON CHRISTMAS DAY.

I SAW THREE SHIPS A-SAILING IN,

ON CHRISTMAS DAY IN THE MORNING.

AND ALL THE BELLS ON EARTH SHALL RING,
ON CHRISTMAS DAY,
ON CHRISTMAS DAY.

AND ALL THE BELLS ON EARTH SHALL RING,
ON CHRISTMAS DAY IN THE MORNING.

(Pause, she waits with the count.)

ON CHRISTMAS DAY,
ON CHRISTMAS DAY.

(Waits another count.)

ON CHRISTMAS DAY IN THE MORNING.

(Pause. SIS waits, then starts to sing on her own. The CHOIRMASTER can't hear this, and he keeps on conducting "Three Ships.")

SIS. SHE WAS ONLY SIXTEEN...
ONLY SIXTEEN,
I LOVED HER SO.

(The CHOIRMASTER points at her.)

SIS. ON CHRISTMAS DAY IN THE MORNING *(Pause)*,
BUT SHE WAS TOO YOUNG TO FALL IN LOVE,
AND I WAS TOO YOUNG TO KNOW.

SHE WAS ONLY SIXTEEN...

All pink and white and fluffy like a marshmallow. So many desirable qualities. She could have been a poster in black sunglasses and blond hair. Her pretty ears admired by the choirmaster. All this at sixteen, the weight of the years not yet showing. Entering the ball in a beaded dress that weighed so much she could hardly stand up straight. But she did, this tiny girl form the Southland, her pupils made small from the flashbulbs. "ON CHRISTMAS DAY, ON CHRISTMAS DAY..." I love to sing; I wish I could be a castrati. Boys get all the fun.

CHOIRMASTER. Kathryn...

SIS. Yes?

CHOIRMASTER. You're not paying attention.

SIS. Sorry... "ON CHRISTMAS DAY..." I guess pretty pink ears don't count for much. How can I possibly pay attention? How can I possibly focus on this little tune when I am so much more fascinating? Those who pass within the area of my magnetism know what I'm talking about. My power extends not just to the length of my arms, but all around me, like a sphere when I pass, in the hallways, lockers, to those who hear my voice. I am a flame, and I bring myself to the unsuspecting moths. Unnaturally and strangely, the power ceases when I'm home. There, my influence stays within here *(She indicates her head.)*, all within. It's all silent in the presence of my mother and father and brother. What they don't realize is that one idea from *this* little mind changes the course of rivers. Not to mention families.

CHOIRMASTER. Kathryn!

SIS. Sorry. *(Pause.)* I know from where my salvation will come. I will give birth to the baby Jesus. The baby Jesus brought to you by Kathryn, the near virgin. I will have to buy swaddling clothes. The sweet baby Jesus, the magician. He will wave his hand, and the dishes will wash themselves; and he will wave his other had, and the water on the dishes will bead up and rise to the heavens in a reverse dish-drying rain. *I* will put them away. And I will sweetly cradle him. People will come to him for miracles, and I will look proudly on. He will grow and become my husband, the true virgin and the near virgin. Both of us perfectly unspoiled, perfectly true. He couldn't work the miracles without me. I would run the minimart and be the inspiration, the wife of Jesus. And at the end of our lives, he would become the baby Jesus again, and I would put him in the swaddling clothes and carry him upward, entering heaven in a beaded dress that weighed so much she could hardly stand up straight. But she did, this tiny girl from the Southland, her pupils made small from the flashbulbs. "ON CHRISTMAS DAY, ON CHRISTMAS DAY. I SAW THREE SHIPS A-SAILING IN, ON CHRISTMAS DAY IN THE MORNING."

CHOIRMASTER. Kathryn, see me after class.
SIS. Finally.

(Lights down.)

Scene 4
YE FAITHFUL

(Lights up. Christmas morning around a tree. Several presents lie under it. A shiny bicycle stands next to it, with a small ribbon around the handlebars. SON enters.)

SON. Yeah!

(DAD enters in his robe.)

DAD. Aren't you going to open it?

(SON unwraps the ribbon.)

SON. Great bicycle! Thanks, Jim!
DAD. Well, that was a nice, little seven-story building you put up, Son.
SON. Did you really think so?
DAD. Well, you're no Frank Lloyd Wright.

(SIS enters.)

SIS. Oh, Christmas! Goddamn us, every one.

(SIS goes over and casually starts tearing open presents. MOM enters, carrying an elaborate Christmas goose on a tray.)

MOM. Good morning!
DAD, SIS, and SON. Not really hungry... I'm full, I had some cereal *(etc.)*.
MOM. *(Cheery:)* Fine!
DAD. How would all you kids like to take a trip to Israel?

(They stare at him.)

DAD. Well, all that history, going back four thousand three hundred twenty-five years. All the big names: Moses, David,

Solomon, Rebecca, Daren the magnificent, Sassafras. See the manger, the palm fronds, go on the rides, see the tablets with the Ten Commandments...

SON. Wow!

DAD. Not the original, of course; those are broken. Since it's Christmas, what if we went through those commandments? Who can name them? Huh?

SON. Thou shalt not kill. Thou shalt not lie...

DAD. Right. Numero uno and numero duo. Don't kill, don't lie. Good advice around the home.

MOM. Don't worship false gods?

DAD. Exactly. Now who can tell me what that means?

SON. Uh...

MOM. Don't know.

(SIS shrugs her shoulders.)

DAD. Well, you know, false gods. Don't worship 'em. What's another?

(They all think.)

SON. How about, Thou shalt not commit adultery?

(DAD goes into a coughing fit.)

DAD. Next.

SIS. Don't change horses in the middle of the stream.

DAD. Good one, peanut. If you start out as one thing, don't end up another thing. People don't like it.

SON. Everything's comin' up roses?

DAD. Good, that's six.
MOM. Honor thy father and thy mother.

(The children cough violently.)

DAD. Good. Well, there you go. Ten commandments.
SIS. How come it's ten?
DAD. Ten is just right. Fourteen, you go, "Enough already." Eight's not enough, make things too easy. But ten, you can't beat ten. That's why he's God. We got ten fingers, ten toes, and through his wisdom, we don't have ten heads. All thought out beforehand. Well, this has been a real fun morning. Oh, by the way, unhappy childhood, happy life. Bye.

(DAD exits. MOM, SIS, and SON wait a beat to see if he's gone. They all begin to speak in upper-class English accents.)

SON. Is he gone?

(The children gather round MOM and kneel.)

SON. Mummy, this has been the most wonderful Christmas ever.
MOM. Well, now off you go to write your thank-you notes. When you're done, you bring them down here, and we'll take each note and set it next to each present you received, and we can make sure you've mentioned each gift in the right way.
SIS. I've already written my thank-you notes. I did them last week.
MOM. How could you have written a thank-you note be-

fore you knew what the gift was?

SIS. I didn't mention the gift.

MOM. Well, we'll have to do them all over again, won't we?

SIS. Yes, Mummy.

(DAD enters. The kids break away from MOM, and they all revert to American accents.)

DAD. Where are my keys?

SON. Over there, Jim.

DAD. *(To SON.)* Christmas or no Christmas, I want that lawn mowed today.

SON. *(American accent:)* I don't wanna!

MOM. *(American accent, faking anger:)* You do as you're told!

SON. *(Faking:)* Oh, Mom!

DAD. Christ! Where are my keys?

SIS. *(American accent.)* In the drawer, Dad.

DAD. *(Picking them up:)* How could they get there?

MOM. The butler must have put them there.

(DAD starts to exit.)

DAD. What butler?

MOM. I mean, I must have put them there. Did you remember your clubs?

(But DAD is gone. The children kneel by MOM again and begin speaking English accents.)

SIS. I have never understood golf.
MOM. Nor I.
SON. Nor I.
MOM. Scottish game, 'tisn't it?
SON. Oh yes, Scottish.
SIS. *Very* Scottish!

(They all chuckle.)

MOM. Oh, Roger!

(An English butler, ROGER, enters carrying a tea tray.)

ROGER. Yes'um?
MOM. Oh. Good. Tea. Has he gone?
ROGER. *(Looks offstage:)* Just driving off now, ma'am.
MOM. We're so naughty!
SIS. You know what I'd like, a big bowl of Wheat-a-Bix!
MOM. On Christmas you can have anything you want. Roger, would you be so kind, one bowl of Wheat-a-Bix.
SON. Oh, I'll have a bowl too!
MOM. Well, me too.
ROGER. Three bowls of Wheet-a-Bix. Clotted cream?
MOM. Of course. Clotted cream, and oh, just bring a big bowl of bacon fat.
ROGER. Mango?
SON. Mango? Oh, Mummy, pretty please!
MOM. Oh, you do love your mango.. We'll take it in the garden. *(Afterthought.)* By the folly.
ROGER. Yes'um.
MOM. Go along, then.

(The children and ROGER exit. MOM is left alone onstage.)

MOM. *(Still speaks with her English accent.)* Voices?
FEMALE VOICE. *(Offstage:)* Yes?
MOM. *(English accent.)* Thank you for these moments.
FEMALE VOICE. Would you like to be Italian?
MOM. Oh no, I'm afraid I would burst. Unless...
FEMALE VOICE. Unless what?
MOM. *(English accent:)* Unless, late at night, when I'm with him, you know, sort of, in bed, well, you know. Maybe just for five minutes.
FEMALE VOICE. You'd like to be Italian for five minutes?
MOM. I was thinking him.
FEMALE VOICE. I see.
MOM. Well, I'll be in the garden by the folly.

(MOM starts to go.)

FEMALE VOICE. One moment. I have an answer to your question.
MOM. *(English accent:)* Which one?
FEMALE VOICE. When he says he loves me, what does he mean?
MOM. *(Normal voice:)* Please.
FEMALE VOICE. He means, if only, if only. If only he could call to you from across a river bank.
MOM. Like Running Bear.
FEMALE VOICE. Yes, as well as Little White Dove. He would dive into the river, swim to you, and drown. He knows this. He cannot come close. He would drown. He knows this.

The water has no value like it does to you; it is only trouble. He does not know the meaning of the water like you do. Standing on the bank, calling to his Little White Dove, with her so small in his vision, he loves her fully. Swimming toward her, his words skipping across to her like flat rocks, he drowns, afraid of what she wants, not knowing what he should be realizing his love was in the words that he shouted while on the bank and not in the small whispers he carries to hand to her.

MOM. Is it ever possible for them not to drown?
FEMALE VOICE. Oh yes.
MOM. What makes the difference?
FEMALE VOICE. When the attraction is chemical.
MOM. Chemical?
FEMALE VOICE. Oh yes. The taste of the skin to the tongue. The touch of the hand to the neck. The shape of the face on the retina. Oh, this is too hard long distance; let me come down to Earth. *(The FEMALE VOICE appears from offstage, wearing a conservative Chanel suit and holding a handbag.)* Can the chemistry of the breath across the lips inhibit the chemistry of bitterness?

(It doesn't strike MOM as unusual that the FEMALE VOICE walks into her living room, looks around.)

MOM. I see. Would you like something?
FEMALE VOICE. *(Now onstage:)* Oh no. I'm just here for a minute...
MOM. Tea?
FEMALE VOICE. Well, maybe just a little.
MOM. Cake?

FEMALE VOICE. No, thanks I'm trying to lose a few pounds. Maybe a small piece. Here, let me help.

(The FEMALE VOICE helps set the table.)

MOM. You were talking about the chemistry of the breath across the lips inhibiting the chemistry of bitterness.

FEMALE VOICE. Oh yeah, what I'm trying to say is: sex is the kicker. It's there to cloud our judgment. Otherwise *nobody* would pair off. Once I slept with a guy just to get him to quit trying to sleep with me.

MOM. I could never do that.

FEMALE VOICE. You're forty. I'm four thousand three hundred twenty-five.

MOM. Any kids?

FEMALE VOICE. I have a girl eleven hundred and a boy eight hundred thirty-five. The eight-hundred thirty-five year old is a terror.

MOM. So how did you get to be omniscient?

FEMALE VOICE. I went to class.

MOM. They have a class? What do you study?

FEMALE VOICE. Every teeny-weeny little thing. We memorize it. Every little rock, every blade of grass. Everything about people, about men, about cats, every type of gravy, every possibility, every potentiality, ducks. It's one class where *et cetera* really means "et cetera."

MOM. That must be hard.

FEMALE VOICE. It is one son of a bitch. You know what one of the questions on the final was?

MOM. What?

FEMALE VOICE. Name everything.

MOM. Wow.

FEMALE VOICE. When I read that question, my mind went blank. Which is a terrible thing when you're asked to name everything.

MOM. What happened?

FEMALE VOICE. Oh, you know, you get through it; I got an eighty-four. Eighty and above is omniscient. Well, I better be going... prom night pimple in Cleveland...

MOM. *(Stops her, concerned:)* So you know everything.

FEMALE VOICE. Somewhat.

MOM. So... what would it be like if I left him?

FEMALE VOICE. You won't believe this, but that was one of the questions on the final. Let's see... you will live in a small cottage. It will be surrounded by a white fence. In the backyard will be many colored flowers. Inside will be small lace doilies like your mother's. You will stand outside on the green lawn, your face up toward the sun; your hands will be outstretched, palms open; and you will speak these words: "What have I done, what have I done, what have I done."

(Slow blackout.)

Scene 5
THE LOGIC OF THE LIE

(The dinner table again, the family of four sitting around. DAD is in the middle of a gold story; the family feigns enjoyment.)

DAD. Phil tees off, lands midway down the fairway but off to the right. With the three wood, I'm about ten yards shy of him but straight down the middle. I can see the flag damn straight up with a trap off to the right. Phil's gotta fly over the trap. *(MOM and family emits sounds of delighted interest.)* What happens? Phil eight irons it and flies the trap; he's on the green. I full swing my nine and land right in the trap!

SON. *(Laughs:)* Oh man!

SIS Wow.

MOM. *(Laughing:)* Man, you don't need a nine iron; you need a hoe!

DAD. So now... Phil on the back of the green putts and rolls right past the hole, and it keeps going to the edge of the fringe.

SIS. *(Laughing:)* Did he use a eight iron for that too?

(The whole family overlaughs.)

DAD. I pop it out of the trap and... *(Starts to laugh.)* ... the damn thing... *(More laughs.)*... rolls right up about ten inches from the hole!

(More laughter from the others.)

DAD. Phil three puts, and I drop it in without hardly looking.

(Really big response from family.)

Mom. Oh... ha ha ha.

(MOM has to drink water and fan herself. The phone rings. MOM answers it.)

SIS. Oh, my God, it's Jeremy!
MOM. Hello? Just a minute. *(To SIS.)* It's Jeremy.
SIS. Tell him I'm not in.
MOM. She's not in right now. *(She hangs up.)* I thought you wanted to talk to him.
SIS. *(Practically sinister:)* He'll call back.

(The table becomes silent as DAD is lost in thought. He hears the sound of the solar wind. Suddenly he stands up, but the rest of the family can't see him.)

DAD. Voice? *(No answer.)* Voice? *(No answer.)* Voices? Voice? Typical, nothing. Left here on my own, with only the images of Washington, Jefferson, and Lincoln. Hello? Hello? I'm living the lie, I know it. Nothing but the rules of the road, the ethics of the lumberjack, the silence of the forest broken only by the sound of the ax getting the job done, the ax never complaining. Truth handed down through the pages of *Redbook* and the *Saturday Evening Post*. Becoming leader and hero, onward and stronger to a better life. I know my feelings cannot tolerate illumination under the hard light, but when seen by the flickering light of a campfire surrounded by the covered wagons heading west, I am a god that walks on Earth. Must be strong, must be strong, and in my silence, I am never wrong. The greater the silence, the greater the strength. And therein is the logic of the lie.
MOM. Butter?

(MOM passes the butter to SON.)

DAD. *(Looks back at MOM:)* Her. Once, with one hand I held her wrists behind her back and kissed her. Once, I entered her like Caesar into Rome. Once, I drank her blood. I would repeat her name in my head; it swam across my vision to exhaustion. I saw it flying toward me and flapping with wings. I exploded it with the letters flying off in all directions. I inverted it; I anagrammed it. Every word she spoke destroyed or created me. She was the tornado, and I was the barn. I remember her in a yellow chair, leaning forward, her underwear ankled, delivering to me the angel's kiss. Now I stand at the foot of her bed and watch her sleep, and silently ask the question "Who are you?" but the question only echoes back upon myself. Oh, I know what she goes through. She aches with desire. She reaches out for nothing, and nothing comes back. She is bound by walls of feeling. They surround me too, but I must reach through the walls and *provide*. There is no providing on a lingering summer's walk; there is no providing in a caress. I have been to the place she wants me to go. *(Bitterly.)* I have seen how the king of feelings, the great god romance seats us in his giant hand and thrusts us upward and slowly turns us under the sky. But it is given to us only for minutes, and we spend the rest of our lives paying for those few moments. Love moves through three stages: attraction, desire, need. The third stage is the place I cannot go.

SON. Jim, can I be excused?

DAD. Finish your meal. *(Back to his soliloquy.)* If I can't be excused, why should he? The denial of my affection will make him strong like me. I would love to feel the emotions I have heard so much about, but I may as well try to reassemble a dandelion. *(He snaps out of it and speaks to the family, back to his vigorous delivery.)* Ninth hole, dog-leg left, can't see the pin. *(The family reacts with oohs and ahs. He turns, walks back to the table.)* I decided to go over the trees, but I hit a bad shot, and it goes straight down the middle of the fairway. I don't say a word! Phil *(Starts chuckling.)*... just slow turns and stares at me with this look!...

(The others laugh. The sound of munching resumes as they fall silent.)

(Slow fade out.)

END OF PLAY

THE ZIG-ZAG WOMAN

THE ZIG-ZAG WOMAN

(The curtain opens on a café set. Upstage center is a woman inside the magic effect The Zig-Zag Woman. It's as though a woman's head, arms, legs, and torso have been separated from one another.)

THE ZIG-ZAG WOMAN. Maybe *now* he'll notice me. *(An OLDER MAN walks out, with a chair. He sits along side THE ZIG-ZAG WOMAN.)* What would you like?
OLDER MAN. I'll just have some coffee.
THE ZIG-ZAG WOMAN. Cream or black?
OLDER MAN. Don't care.
THE ZIG-ZAG WOMAN. Here you are, here's your coffee.

(THE ZIG-ZAG WOMAN doesn't hand him the coffee; it just appears. A convention.)

OLDER MAN. Thank you. *(He takes a sip of imaginary coffee. Pause.)* May I pay you a compliment?

THE ZIG-ZAG WOMAN. All right.

OLDER MAN. It's really nice the way your head is separated from your body like that.

THE ZIG-ZAG WOMAN. Thank you.

OLDER MAN. Most women, their heads are *on* their bodies. You don't often see one separated like yours.

THE ZIG-ZAG WOMAN. Well, thank you. *(To audience, pointing and gesturing with her exposed hands.)* You should know this is not the one. *(To OLDER MAN:)* Will there be anything else?

OLDER MAN. Could I ask you one more question?

THE ZIG-ZAG WOMAN. Please.

OLDER MAN. Why is your head separated from your body?

THE ZIG-ZAG WOMAN. I'm trying to meet someone.

OLDER MAN. In my day, they used Chanel Number 5. What's the reason for meeting this person.

THE ZIG-ZAG WOMAN. I want to be in love.

OLDER MAN. Ah yes.

THE ZIG-ZAG WOMAN. All day long, I look into strangers' eyes and ask them what they want. I wait for them to ask me what I want, but they never do. I set the plates down in front of them, and for a second, I close my eyes and wait for a touch on the hand that never comes.

OLDER MAN. Just when you think love is dead, it is waiting for you like a crouching panther. But easy takes the step, easy takes the step.

THE ZIG-ZAG WOMAN. Yes.

OLDER MAN. Remember the dawn breaks.

THE ZIG-ZAG WOMAN. The dawn breaks?

OLDER MAN. The dawn breaks everything, including the mood from the night before.

THE ZIG-ZAG WOMAN. I see.

OLDER MAN. Would you like me to slide you back together?

THE ZIG-ZAG WOMAN. *(Looks offstage to see if anyone is coming:)* Maybe just for a minute.

(THE OLDER MAN stands up and slides her middle back together. THE ZIG-ZAG WOMAN gets out of the box and investigates her stomach.)

THE ZIG-ZAG WOMAN. That feels better.

(THE ZIG-ZAG WOMAN sets a candle on each of the tables and lights the candles.)

OLDER MAN. The things you gals put yourselves through. Now, me? I've been in love with the same woman my whole life. She's gone now, but not a day goes by that I don't think about her.

THE ZIG-ZAG WOMAN. What was she like?

OLDER MAN. Well, she had a laugh that could spin your head around, and a personality as unpredictable as a ricochet. She could write, sing, and draw, and she issued a declaration of independence every time she entered a room. She was smart as a whip yet could sit down intensely with the morning crossword and not get one. She brightened my life in a way I never could for myself. Her hair was practically edible. Joy issued from her eyes and hands and her walk, and she could sit like Buddah and speak to the fourth place in your heart.

THE ZIG-ZAG WOMAN. You must miss her.

OLDER MAN. I do.

THE ZIG-ZAG WOMAN. How long has she been gone?

OLDER MAN. Twenty-three years. *(Pause.)* Divorced me, married an actor. In the beginning of something, its ending is foretold, and we met in an elevator going down. After she left, in my travels I would sit in hotel lobbies expecting her to appear, telling me what a mistake she'd made. I would land at airports, thinking that she got my flight number and would be waiting for me. When I went to a show, I would buy two tickets in case she had found out where I was and quietly joined me, nothing having to be said. I never figured out why she went away, but I did figure out this: love is a promise delivered already broken.

THE ZIG-ZAG WOMAN. I should go back in the box.

OLDER MAN. Here, let me help.

(The OLDER MAN helps her back into the box. While the box is in the closed position, he opens the stomach window and tickles THE ZIG-ZAG WOMAN. She laughs.)

THE ZIG-ZAG WOMAN. Just slide my middle out. *(The OLDER MAN does this.)* Thank you.

(A second man, the MIDDLE MAN, enters. Midthirties, brassy and loud. Texan. He sits.)

MIDDLE MAN. Oh, hell with it, I'll have a piece of pie.

THE ZIG-ZAG WOMAN. *(Quickly:)* Here you are.

MIDDLE MAN. Today is my anniversary.

THE ZIG-ZAG WOMAN. Mine, too. Two years with nobody. How about you?

MIDDLE MAN. Twelve years. Twelve years with the wifey.

She recently cut her hair short. Looks good. Last night I put my head between her legs, and it was still paradise. I hope I didn't offend you.

THE ZIG-ZAG WOMAN. *(To audience:)* By the way, this is not him either.

MIDDLE MAN. Tough debate. Married or single. Single brings a sadness, but sadness has its own perfection. Marriage brings a misery of a rare kind, the kind that loves company. *(He looks at THE ZIG-ZAG WOMAN:)* You look like a girl in a fix.

THE ZIG-ZAG WOMAN. A bit of one. The four-wall kind.

MIDDLE MAN. What do you mean?

THE ZIG-ZAG WOMAN. The staring-at-four-walls kind.

MIDDLE MAN. Well, you've got to get it together, babe. There's no four walls inside your head. You just get yourself a personality, that's all. You put two women next to each other, one with a personality and one without, you go for the one with the personality every time. Unless the other one is wearing a red dress. But that's the mistake a lotta guys make. I mean, that red dress comes off. The personality doesn't. So here's what you do: You get yourself one of those self-help books. You know, nine ways to do this, seven ways to do that. You memorize that stuff, tell it to people, and they think you're a genius. They think *you live by it,* but really you're just going home and whacking off to a record, banging your head against a headboard as the TV sends numbing rays to your groin.

THE ZIG-ZAG WOMAN. Have you noticed that I'm ripped apart?

MIDDLE MAN. Oh yeah, but I didn't know if it was some cosmetic surgery or what. You know, the latest thing. Didn't know if I should mention it. At the parties I go to, you could spend all night not mentioning things. At the parties I go to, there's enough hacked-off flesh to create another party somewhere else. Probably a more fun party, since all that flesh would have to be reanimated by some scientist using pig brains, which would create at least *something*. Is this some kind of beauty thing, like a nose ring?

THE ZIG-ZAG WOMAN. This is just a displacement of the heart.

MIDDLE MAN. Ah yes. But that can be beautiful too. *(He opens the stomach window in the Zig-Zag box and tickles her.)* Here, let me be a momentary salve. *(He slides he middle; she gets out of the box.)* Take the first wife. Crazy as a map of London. Her heart was displaced into the next state. Made her attractive. Every night was like drawing to an inside straight: all or nothing. Ecstasy or agony. She shot herself with a twenty-two. Dumb. Took nine days to die. If you're going to shoot yourself, you gotta use something big like a cannon. Otherwise, you could lay around for years on your own bathroom schedule. Anyway, she lay there comatose, then suddenly popped into consciousness and told me this. I mean these were her dying words; she looked me straight in the eye and said, "I would assign every lie a color: yellow when they were innocent, pale blue when they sailed over you like the sky, red because I knew they drew blood. And then there was the black like. That's the worst of all." She said, "A black lie was when I told you the truth."

THE ZIG-ZAG WOMAN. How can the truth be a lie?

MIDDLE MAN. That's what I asked her, and here's what she said: "I told you the truth not to tell you the truth, but because I knew the truth would hurt you." By the way, this is so typical of her. You didn't get dying words; you got a dying essay. Then I asked her why did she do it, why did she shoot herself, and she said, "The joy of life juts out of me like the Matterhorn, but the pain of life looms over me like Everest." Then she dropped her head down on the pillow dramatically, like she died. I thought she died too, but they told me she actually died three hours later. Not from what you think. Diabetes. They said she could have lived with the bullet in her head. In fact, it was lodged in the right side of her brain, and they said the only consequence was it would probably make her draw better. Drama queen. Am I talkin' too much?

THE ZIG-ZAG WOMAN. More pie?

MIDDLE MAN. Pie. Pie. That reminds me of something. I don't know why. *(He stands, lost in his memory.)* I was eighteen. I was traveling in Italy with my girlfriend. She was seventeen. She was seventeen. We had about six months of experience between us. We had no money. I can't remember how we got there. But can you imagine? Eighteen in Italy with nothing but T-shirts and a bag. Not one word of Italian. One watch between us. No tickets, no reservations. A compass. A compass... we thought that would be useful. Like we would suddenly be helped if we knew north. It was August like nobody's business. So hot you could fry eggs in the *air.* We decided to sleep in a park next to the Coliseum. Cars all night long. We went to an Italian market and bought a bottle of white wine. Screw top. We drank it; it tasted bad, but we got drunk, drunk in the park. Sleeping bags, love. Love. The night. Eighteen. We saved the bottle, kept it with us, took it back with us. Later we were told it was olive oil.

(A YOUNG MAN enters, full of fire.)

YOUNG MAN. I'll have six cheeseburgers, five Cokes, one Sprite, two shrimp salads, four iced teas, and three bags of fries.

THE ZIG-ZAG WOMAN. To go?

(The YOUNG MAN never looks at THE ZIG-ZAG WOMAN.)

YOUNG MAN. No, I'll eat it here.
THE ZIG-ZAG WOMAN. Here you are.

(The food appears.)

YOUNG MAN. American food. Yes! I just came back from Italy? I was with a girl; she's seventeen. She went to Italy to get a face-lift and abortion. Plus they can do a twelve-step program there in eight steps. She got busted coming back trying to take a gun on the plane. They let me get on 'cause they couldn't link me to her, even though she was staring into my face and screaming my name in the waiting lounge. I got bumped up to first class on the way back, so all in all, it was a pretty good trip. But I did learn this, though: no more girlfriends that I meet on the street. Hey, guess what? I woke up the other day and had a brilliant flash of insight.

(The YOUNG MAN finds this amusing, then goes back to eating.)

OLDER MAN. *(After a pause:)* Well, what the hell was it?
YOUNG MAN. Sorry?
OLDER MAN. What was the insight?
YOUNG MAN. Oh, well, here goes. I figured this: I'm

twenty-one years old.
OLDER MAN. I know what you mean.
MIDDLE MAN. Keep talkin', kid.
YOUNG MAN. And how much could I really know.
OLDER MAN. Very wise.
MIDDLE MAN. A wise old owl at twenty-one.
YOUNG MAN. I figure a lot. I probably know a lot.

(The OLDER MAN and the MIDDLE MAN look at each other.)

OLDER MAN. He doesn't understand.
MIDDLE MAN. No way.
YOUNG MAN. I came up with this: Every emotion is consumed by its opposite. Every ounce of pleasure is balanced by an equal amount of disaster. Generosity breeds contempt; power breeds weakness. Agony leads to a greater appreciation of bliss. You love your friends, they start dying; when your friends start dying, you take more chances with our own life. Every ache you feel makes its inverse more possible. And that is the ecology of joy and pain.
THE ZIG-ZAG WOMAN. *(To audience:)* You should know that this is him.
MIDDLE MAN. *(Snaps his fingers:)* Her nickname was pie. That's what reminded me of her. Sorry, go ahead.
YOUNG MAN. *(Stands, goes downstage of the Zig-Zag box:)* I'm tryin' to combine the both. The full life. The good with the...

(The YOUNG MAN indicates the others to finish his sentence.)

MIDDLE MAN. Bad.

YOUNG MAN. The dark with the...
OLDER MAN. Light.
YOUNG MAN. The yin with the...

(There is a long pause while the OLDER MAN and the MIDDLE MAN look at each other.)

OLDER MAN. Good?
YOUNG MAN. The yin with the...
MIDDLE MAN. Uh... yellow?
YOUNG MAN. The yin... with the...
OLDER MAN. Hey, you, bub?
YOUNG MAN. The yin with the...
THE ZIG-ZAG WOMAN. Yang.

(The YOUNG MAN snaps his fingers and points, but does not look at her.)

YOUNG MAN. Right-o.
THE ZIG-ZAG WOMAN. What about love?
YOUNG MAN. Love? When I feel myself falling in love, I go buy a boomerang instead. At least with a boomerang, something comes back to you. Unless, of course, she were zig-zagged. If she were zig-zagged, there you go, that would be a girl I could love forever.

(The OLDER MAN and the MIDDLE MAN look at the ZIG-ZAG WOMAN, who is out of her box. She and they rush into the box. The YOUNG MAN still faces forward but won't look.)

YOUNG MAN. No middle... arm a mile from her torso... now we're talkin'. We'd walk down the street side by side by side. We'd live in a little cottage with a fireplace; just her and me and three little zig-zag babies...
MIDDLE MAN. Hello?
THE ZIG-ZAG WOMAN. Hello?
OLDER MAN. Hello?
YOUNG MAN. Not right now, I'm thinkin' about the Zig-Zag Woman.
OLDER MAN. What it takes to turn someone's head today.

(The OLDER MAN opens his suitcase and retrieves the Twister: the Twister is a magician's trick where a person's head appears to twist fully around. He walks over to the YOUNG MAN and puts it on his head.)

YOUNG MAN. Excuse me?
OLDER MAN. Excuse *me*.

(The OLDER MAN then twists the YOUNG MAN's head around, 360 degrees. The OLDER MAN realizes he's twisted it too far and moves the YOUNG MAN's head around again to 180 degrees. Now the YOUNG MAN stares directly at THE ZIG-ZAG WOMAN.)

THE ZIG-ZAG WOMAN. Hi.
YOUNG MAN. Hi. My God, you're coming apart.
THE ZIG-ZAG WOMAN. You're twisted.

(The YOUNG MAN walks toward her—backwards, of course.)

MIDDLE MAN. My wife has no head. And you know what, she gets around just fine.

OLDER MAN. My wife could eat fire, and I loved her for it.

YOUNG MAN. *(Walks toward her—backwards, of course:)* Would you like to go to a movie?

THE ZIG-ZAG WOMAN. Yes, I would.

YOUNG MAN. How would we do that?

MIDDLE MAN. Here.

(The MIDDLE MAN walks over to the YOUNG MAN and untwists his head, leaving the Twister box on him.)

YOUNG MAN. Man, that was invigorating.

(The YOUNG MAN takes the Woman's zig-zagged hand and starts to push her off the stage, leaving the two other men alone.)

YOUNG MAN. Want to get a snack first?

THE ZIG-ZAG WOMAN. *(As they exit:)* I could go for some pretzels.

OLDER MAN. In the beginning of something, its ending is foretold.

MIDDLE MAN. How do you think they will end?

OLDER MAN. That's an easy one.

(The OLDER MAN waves his hand over the candle; there is a small explosion of fire.)

MIDDLE MAN. Well, good night.

(The MIDDLE MAN exits. The OLDER MAN sits a minute, then brings the MIDDLE MAN's chair over to his table. He adjusts it, so a second person could join him. He sits carefully back in his own chair, adjusts the second chair again, then hopefully looks offstage toward the door and waits.)

(Slow fade to black.)

END OF PLAY

PATTER FOR THE FLOATING LADY

pat.ter *n.* **1**. Glib, rapid speech, as of a magician, a salesperson, or a comedian.

PATTER FOR THE FLOATING LADY was first produced by the New York Stage and Film Company and the Powerhouse Theater at Vassar in association with RJK Productions. The cast included:

Bill Irwin
Carrie Preston
Kimberly Williams

Director: **Barry Edelstein**
Stage Manager: **Sandi Johnson**

....

PATTER FOR THE FLOATING LADY's original New York production was by the New York Shakespeare Festival, George C. Wolfe, Producer, with the following cast:

Magician: ....Don McManus
Angie: ....Amelia Campbell
Assistant: ....Carol Kane

Director: **Barry Edelstein**
Scenic Designer: **Thomas Lynch**
Lighting Designer: **Donald Holder**
Costume Designer: **Laura Cunningham**
Sound Designer: **Red Ramona**
Production Stage Manager: **James Latus**

PATTER FOR THE FLOATING LADY

(Curtain opens to reveal a stage set with a magic theme. Slow, melodic music plays. The MAGICIAN enters. He is forty, dressed in magician's clothes.)

MAGICIAN. On my recent trip to India, I traveled in a small village far, far away form civilization. I had heard about an Indian fakir with extraordinary powers who lived in this village. One of his powers was the ability to levitate a woman, to cause her to float in the air with no visible means of support. I happened to see a demonstration of this in person, outdoors, on a hot summer day. This fakir, or mystic, took two bamboo poles and stuck them into the sand. Then, he looked toward his assistant, a very modest woman—modest but, I must say, very beautiful in her plainness—and hypnotized her. She then sat in the lotus position between the two poles, which she lightly touched with her fingers. There was no noise in the crowd who stood motionless in a semicircle around them. Then, slowly, inch by inch, she rose up; she was suspended in the air. The circumstances were so simple, there was no question of trickery. As I stood there watching her float in the hot, desert air, I said to myself, "That's something I'd like to do to Angie." Angie?

(ANGIE enters. She is probably twenty-five, offbeat looking in her clothes; wears glasses, but that's because she's quietly hip. She's got something, but it's understated. She stands at the side of the stage.)

MAGICIAN. Angie plays the violin; she has a busy life, and she isn't going for this trick very much, you can imagine... *(To ANGIE:)* Angie, would you mind changing into your costume now?

(Annoyed, ANGIE exits.)

MAGICIAN. *(Checks to make sure she's gone:)* You have to understand that when I see Angie, I experience a bright yellow flash of desire. And I thought if I could give her this, if I could suspend her in space, this would be my exchange for the nights I laid on top of her, she experiencing nothing. This would be my gift to her, even if I do it with black velvet and trickery, she won't mind, since she understands, as I do, that with the exception of a few profound and fleeting moments in our lives, everything we say is a lie.

(The MAGICIAN goes offstage and wheels on the floating-lady equipment.)

MAGICIAN. My love for Angie has never moved in the two years I've known her. This drove her insane. I tried to bury how deeply I felt for her, but I was weak and my eyes betrayed me. She told me once that sometimes when she was with me, she could feel my happiness drain out of me; it was true, since she could destroy me by answering the phone. The irony is that she loved me. That's what I couldn't leave alone: "How much?" "How much?" I needed the answer constantly, not just once, not just with her touch in the yard in the night with the dog, not in the morning over coffee with a look, but during her excursions into her own life, which I knew nourished her love for me. Tonight I want to levitate her, not for me, but for her. I would like her to know how it feels to have no attachments. I would like her to know how it feels to have no attachments, yet her freedom is mine. The power from my hands holding her suspended, even if only a few feet above ground. I don't think she wanted to cause me pain. She wanted to speak painful things to me, and I would deflect them; this would be her freedom. If we could have graphed our happiness, its silhouette would have been the image of the Himalayas. Up and down. Zig-zagging with ragged angles. She used to whisper her secrets directly in my ear; I now hear about her from fourth best friends. Tonight I give her this pathetic gift. This is the limit of my imagination, and my only solace is that no poem, no song, no psalm from David himself could have brought her to me. And I know that tonight when she has been levitated four feet closer to the stars, she will walk out the door and not look back. I know this, so please don't feel for me; the pain is mine to play with. Angie?

(ANGIE enters. This time in a different dress, a sort of fairy-magician's assistant-showbiz thing. ANGIE holds her magician's assistant smile and poses for the audience, looks over at him out of the corner of her eye. She stands at the side of the stage; the MAGICIAN lights incense and begins to wave his hands to hypnotize her. Music.)

MAGICIAN. Your eyelids are heavy...
ANGIE. Oh, please.
MAGICIAN. They are very, very heavy.
ANGIE. No, they're not.
MAGICIAN. Oh yeah, sleep. Let yourself drift, drift over the memories, our night in the tropics with your skin cool as an orchid. Black sky over us, pinholes of light punching through its canopy, torches around us, the white smear of the Milky Way extending from Pole to Pole and the light touch of alcohol covering us with is thin oil. Let's float over the night we dreamed of loving each other... the night we knew we could never be, yet we merged like ghosts, translucent one on another.

(ANGIE collapses, hypnotized. The MAGICIAN catches her, lifts her up, steadies her.)

MAGICIAN. There were five hundred nights from beginning to end, five hundred sunrises bearing the name "Angie." Five hundred days ago, I met her and caught the scent of the wild rose, the wild rose with an iron stem.

(ANGIE is hypnotized. The MAGICIAN lets her go; she is able to stand on her own. Momentarily, her eyes open; then softly, she begins to speak:)

ANGIE. I remember you holding me like I was a baby lamb, so safe, like we were suspended in space. Nothing to stop the movement flowing forward. God, it was beautiful, but time ran out.

(The MAGICIAN is at the opposite side of the stage.)

MAGICIAN. *(Speaking antiphonally:)* Time ran out.
ANGIE. Like the biorhythms of the pyramids.
MAGICIAN. Like the biorhythms of the pyramids.
ANGIE. Measured on the ancient scale.
MAGICIAN. The ancient scale.
ANGIE. A match that was written in code.
MAGICIAN. A mismatch made in heaven.
ANGIE. My love for you should have had no limit.
MAGICIAN. Yes, it should have.
ANGIE. But it didn't.
MAGICIAN. It should have, but it didn't.
ANGIE. It stopped at my fingertips.
MAGICIAN. Mine stopped at Saturn.
ANGIE. Do you have a cigarette?
MAGICIAN. No.
ANGIE. Are you sure?
MAGICIAN. I'm sure.
ANGIE. God, I want a cigarette.
MAGICIAN. *(Trying to get her back on track:)* The ancient scale.
ANGIE. Oh yeah, the ancient scale.
ANGIE. *(Back in the trance:)* Ah...
MAGICIAN. The metaphor of the rectangle. Crazy love. Love intensified. Love so singular it had no opposite. Can you remember?
ANGIE. Yes.
MAGICIAN. Angie, would you let me take you back to it?
ANGIE. I'm afraid.
MAGICIAN. Will you go back?

ANGIE. Yes.

(The MAGICIAN takes ANGIE over to the device, sits her on it, and ties two scarves to her wrists, one to the pole. The MAGICIAN makes magic gestures. ANGIE begins to float upward slowly. Halfway up the poles, she stops.)

MAGICIAN. Are you there?
ANGIE. Yes.
MAGICIAN. Can you see us?
ANGIE. Yes.
MAGICIAN. Was there anything you loved about me? That you remember?
ANGIE. Oh yes. I loved you. So many things. The safety. The words exchanged. Letters. I would cough and the phone would ring and it would be you asking me if I was all right. You could imitate me and make me laugh. You would buy me a little thing. When I made spaghetti for you, you were so grateful, Pavarotti himself couldn't have made better spaghetti. We were at a restaurant and a woman came up to you, flirting and right there in front of her, you laced your fingers between mine, showing her who you loved. But the most powerful was the tennis shoe. My God, I cried. After our week in the tropics—where we collapsed, ended—a month later, not having spoken, you sent me a tennis shoe. I looked at it for days, not knowing why you sent it. Then one morning, barefoot, not knowing why, I slipped my foot into it. Sand. Grains of sand still in it from seven thousand miles away; each one the size of a memory. I will love you forever for that second. I cried. I cried for us. But when we fell apart, you didn't understand that I would be back. That if you let me have my life, I would

be with you forever. Now, I see other people.
MAGICIAN. Don't hurt me, I'll drop you.
ANGIE. Sometimes I give myself to them.
MAGICIAN. I'll drop you...
ANGIE. You can't.
MAGICIAN. I can. You're floating under my power.
ANGIE. No, I'm not, I just make you think I am.

(A female ASSISTANT walks out with a hoop, in another magician's assistant getup. She tosses the hoop to the MAGICIAN, then removes one of the poles holding up ANGIE. The MAGICIAN tries to prevent her, "No!" but he's too late. The ASSISTANT has the pole, but ANGIE remains aloft. The MAGICIAN is amazed. The ASSISTANT then passes the hoop around ANGIE.)

MAGICIAN. Who are you?
ASSISTANT. I'm working for Angie.
MAGICIAN. *(Bewildered:)* How's she floating?
ASSISTANT. Just don't worry about it.
MAGICIAN. Hey, just get the hell out of here.
ASSISTANT. Don't you think you've done enough?
MAGICIAN. Just go. I can handle Angie.
ASSISTANT. And a bulldozer can handle a Tiffany lamp.
MAGICIAN. You're fired!
ASSISTANT. *(To audience:)* He read her diary. Can you believe it?
MAGICIAN. Well, thank you. Okay, so I read her diary.
ASSISTANT. He picked it up and read it while she was away.
MAGICIAN. She left it out.

ASSISTANT. She left it out in a locked desk.

MAGICIAN. She left the key out.

ASSISTANT. She left the key out in her purse.

MAGICIAN. She left her purse out.

ASSISTANT. Her purse was in her apartment that you had to drive to.

MAGICIAN. She asked for it.

ASSISTANT. Bad.

MAGICIAN. Like I'm supposed to accidentally find a key in her purse to a locked drawer that I know contains her diary and not have my curiosity piqued?

ASSISTANT. Bad.

MAGICIAN. A moment of weakness.

ASSISTANT. More like a lifetime of weakness revealed in a moment.

MAGICIAN. Who are you?

ASSISTANT. *(Suddenly quite serious:)* I'm the part of Angie you don't like. I'm the part of her that would rather kill you than sleep with you. I'm the one who didn't call you at midnight on New Year's Eve after I told you I would. You moron. I'm the one who could create a distance between us that was so subtle only your subconscious knew it was there. I'm the one who took you in my naked arms, made love to you, needed you, and simultaneously let you know that I was not yours. I'm the one who took your faults and wrapped them around your own throat.

MAGICIAN. After everything I gave her.

ASSISTANT. What you gave her was confinement in the name of continuous and abiding love.

(Suddenly, ANGIE's head raises.)

ASSISTANT. Listen, she wants to say something.

(ANGIE begins to rise suddenly, upward to the top of the poles. The movement stops.)

ASSISTANT. Listen. Here comes your misery, wrapped in the most beautiful thing on Earth.

ANGIE. Dream. There is a dream inside me and a corona surrounding me. The dream is of a bright star in eclipse, and its corona shimmers magnetically. You saw it. I love you for seeing it. It drew you to me, into the dream. But I needed time, and you didn't have time. Everything you said and did, every touch at night in bed, every act of kindness, every generosity, every loving comment had this sentence attached: Maybe now she'll love me. And it made you weak. And if I'm not going to love someone strong, why love at all?

MAGICIAN. Why didn't you tell me?

ANGIE. I needed you to have already known it. You should have seen that to let you in hurt me, because you wanted the part of me you cannot have; you wanted the part that no one should have of another person. *(She is at the zenith.)* And I will have my dreams remain inside me, for me, and if you had let them be, they would have been for you too. So now I wait for a man my own age who will stand before me at arms length, and I will hand him unimaginable joy, and he will not move forward, or move back. Then I will hand him unimaginable pain. And he will stand neither moving forward nor moving back. Then and only then, I will slit myself from here to here *(she indicates a vertical line from her neck to her abdomen)*, open my skin and close him into me.

MAGICIAN. My God.

(ANGIE descends rapidly. The ASSISTANT helps her down and leaves the stage.)

ANGIE. I'm gone.

(ANGIE walks off the stage.)

MAGICIAN. Angie!

(She is gone. The MAGICIAN contemplates for a moment, then reaches in the air and produces a cigarette, holding it between his fingers. He looks back smugly where ANGIE exited.)

MAGICIAN. I see a large, carved face in front of me with tiki lips, something Hawaiian, wearing a crown of leaves, and he speaks these words: Love makes us godlike with this exception: after the Crucifixion, we have to roll away our own stone. *(He takes a puff or pauses.)* And now, is there a woman from the audience who would like to assist me?

(Blackout.)

END OF PLAY

GUILLOTINE

GUILLOTINE

(Curtain up to reveal an empty stage with an eight foot guillotine on it. A man, SALESMAN, enters, waits. A second man, CUSTOMER, enters.)

CUSTOMER. I'd like to buy a Guillotine.
SALESMAN. Is this for home or office?
CUSTOMER. Home.
SALESMAN. For what purpose are you getting it?
CUSTOMER. Self-protection.
SALESMAN. We have a nice one here. Let me show you.

(The SALESMAN touches a lever by its side, the blade falls.)

CUSTOMER. My, that's impressive.

(The SALESMAN raises the blade and secures it.)

SALESMAN. Yes, it's quite a little beauty.

(The CUSTOMER goes over to examine the machine. He starts

to touch the lever that releases the blade.)

SALESMAN. Don't touch that! It's very sensitive... dangerous.
CUSTOMER. I see. Well, this looks like a pretty good guillotine. I'll take it.

(Blackout.)

(CUSTOMER enters in front of curtain with a cellular phone in hand.)

CUSTOMER. Hi baby, it's me... You're breaking up... I can hardly hear you... Tell the maid that the lever on the Guillotine is very sensitive... I can't hear you... Tell the maid that the lever is very sensi... Damn I lost her!

(The lights dim. When they come up again, the guillotine is now center stage with several home furnishings around it. A sofa, a table and a chair. A FRENCH MAID enters, around 25 in the full French Maid uniform. She has a feather duster. Perhaps she is singing to herself. She starts to dust the chair. She's very good and very thorough. She dusts the top, turns it over and dusts the bottom. Next, the table. She dusts the top, as well as every leg. Then crawls underneath to get to every nook and cranny. She goes over to the guillotine and starts dusting. Dusting, dusting, dusting. She wants to clean every bit. She starts to clean the slot for the head, wants to get it from another angle, and puts her head in it. Now she starts to dust over by the lever we were warned

about, slowly inching toward. Dust, dust, dust. The duster gets to the lever, she cleans it and the blade falls, cutting off her head.)

(Curtain.)

(A voice comes over the sound system:)

ANNOUNCER. Tomorrow night, the role of the maid will be played by Susan Gelman. The audience is requested not to reveal the ending of the play, especially to Susan Gelman.

(Lights out.)

END OF PLAY